OPERA CAVALCADE

It is a noble house; and indeed I love it well.

OPERA
CAVALCADE

THE STORY OF THE METROPOLITAN

PUBLISHED BY THE METROPOLITAN OPERA GUILD INC.
NEW YORK

EDWARD JOHNSON, By Steichen

FOREWORD

To BE LOVED, great music must be understood. Intelligent appreciation is the key which unlocks the door to a world of sound with unlimited possibilities for enjoyment. In this world, opera takes an important place. Yet, of all music, opera is perhaps the least understood by the general public.

It is difficult to write about great music. The clear, bird-like beauty of a coloratura aria, and the grandeur of a Liebestod do not yield readily to a description in words. Yet words may lead to their deeper appreciation —make clear the conception and purpose of the composer, and reveal the capacity of the artist. Words can portray to those unfamiliar with the history of music the tradition which is the product of more than a hundred years of opera in America; words can remind those steeped in this tradition of past glories and future possibilities.

It is the necessity for such words that has led to the publication of *Opera Cavalcade*. With the developments of the past few years, interest in operatic music is no longer limited to a group or a section of the country. It is no longer exclusively a metropolitan taste. It belongs to the entire country. Public interest has been aroused, not only in opera, but in the manner of producing it, and the personalities of those who interpret it.

Opera Cavalcade, within the limitations of a short book, attempts to satisfy this interest. It endeavors to set forth something of the history and tradition of this great opera house, its ideals, its ambitions, its personalities, both on stage and behind the scenes; and something of the study and work and effort which go into the production of grand opera. It is a book not only for musicians and opera goers, but for the curious who perhaps for the first time will penetrate the veil of awe which has always surrounded the subject, and discover grand opera, not as a remote wonder, but as an ever-present pleasure of everyday living.

Opera Cavalcade represents one more splendid effort of the Opera Guild to interpret opera to the public. We who share the final responsibility for the Metropolitan Opera commend it most highly, believing it will perform a valuable service in incorporating great music as a vital factor into American life.

AMERICA is entering her golden age of opera!

It has been almost a hundred years since the first zealous group of opera lovers decided that opera, in America at least, had passed its zenith, and that never again would performances such as those given in the old Park Theatre be heard in this country. This group watched the closing of the unsuccessful Astor Place Opera House in 1847 with more satisfaction, perhaps, than regret. They murmured dolefully, "It will never be what it was in the old days," when an opera season was announced for the Academy of Music in 1854.

The splendid Academy performances won new devotees who were adamant in their refusal to admit the merit of any newcomer. When a greater opera house—The Metropolitan—was announced for 1883, there were many who wagged their heads and repeated the verbal epitaph, "It won't be what it was in the old days."

Thus it has been throughout the history of opera in America. Each new development, each generation of artists has produced a new "golden age" and a new group of those who say it will be the last.

But today, in truth, America is entering her golden age of opera, and she is entering it because of the changed attitude of the American people. A nation, like an individual, finds its soul slowly. Spiritual consciousness is a product of maturity, and with maturity comes the wisdom of understanding that true culture is not a veneer to be superficially acquired, but a way of life—both for an individual and a people. Those who in recent years predicted that grand opera would soon be a thing of the past, were perhaps unaware of America's increasing maturity. They had not realized that opera was exerting an increasing influence on many thousands of people outside of the few privileged to attend actual performances. They failed to consider that great voices had become familiar to the entire country through phonograph recordings; that even as America rollickingly repeated "Mr. Cohen on the Telephone," it was also making tentative humming experiments with *Butterfly's* "Un Bel Di" and the lusty Toreador Song from *Carmen*.

And they reckoned wholly without the radio! For radio has brought opera to millions whose vague nostalgia for good music has been crystallized through education into a discerning demand for fine performances of operas ranging from *Gianni Schicchi* to *Götterdämmerung*. Radio has provided America with an opportunity for the understanding without which full enjoyment of opera is impossible.

America has approached opera slowly, cautiously, first with suspicion, then with curiosity, then with interest and finally with enthusiasm. Opera to the average American is no longer merely a social occasion. No longer is it a meaningless surge of music with long drawn out action and words in a foreign tongue. If to some it is still a puzzle, it is one which the average listener knows he can solve for himself. Operatic music is being felt and understood. It is becoming part of the national consciousness. Slowly, but steadily and with great satisfaction, America is becoming opera minded.

Inevitably the old and familiar cycle will persist. The great of the past are supplanted by the great of the present who will be replaced by the great of the future. But the Metropolitan, schooled by experience and enriched by tradition, is pledged as always to provide the greatest available opera company in the world. And today, with a growing and eager audience critically appreciative of that company, the picture is complete. America can now enjoy a truly—Golden Age of Opera.

Meet The Metropolitan!

One Caruso doesn't make an opera. One first night doesn't make a season!

The Metropolitan Opera does not consist only of the obvious elements of its scheduled weeks of magnificent music-pageantry. Into each season goes much which is concealed from the casual observer, tremendously detailed preparation which seems far removed from the actual performance. Into it go pride in the past and confidence in the future of a great institution, and the coordinated hard work of hundreds of persons. Into it go a year, two, three years of planning and preparation; sets that have been especially designed, built or reconditioned; repertory that has been carefully scheduled; benefit performances that have been wisely chosen; artists who have been engaged; repairs which have been made to house, to stage, to costumes, to temperaments.

A great operatic organization must combine these elements:

ARTISTS
: The quality of the voices, the personality and character of the principal singers play a major part in the success of an opera company.

TRADITION
: A great opera company arises out of a great history. Pride in the background of the organization and its past achievements is an incentive to superlative work.

BUSINESS MANAGEMENT
: Tickets—money—contracts—if possible a balanced budget. The business side of opera must operate with the humane efficiency of a modern corporation yet never with the sacrifice of artistic effect.

BACKSTAGE MECHANICS
: The opera goes off smoothly, it has beauty and realism because several hundred people work backstage to make it so.

CHORUS
: A coordinated musical unit, capable of producing background music and colorful stage pictures is necessary as a setting for opera.

ORCHESTRA
: An organization must respond as one instrument to a conductor whose duty it is to weave voice and accompaniment into a perfect whole.

AUDIENCE
: An intelligently appreciative audience inspires fine singing and memorable performances. And opera, to be fully enjoyed, must be fully understood.

IDEAL
: An opera company without an ideal is like an artist without a soul: it may produce music, even good music; but opera is not merely good music. . . .

Consideration of these elements constitutes *Opera Cavalcade—the Story of the Metropolitan.*

Genesis of a Metropolitan Career

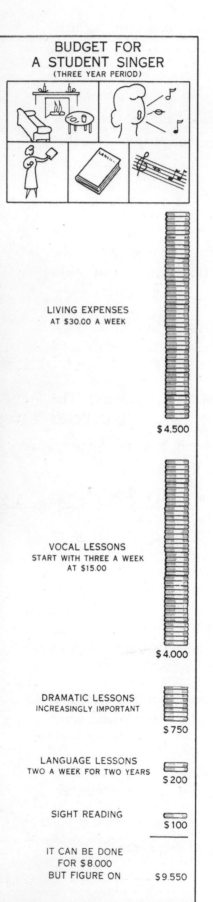

BUDGET FOR A STUDENT SINGER
(THREE YEAR PERIOD)

LIVING EXPENSES
AT $30.00 A WEEK
$4,500

VOCAL LESSONS
START WITH THREE A WEEK
AT $15.00
$4,000

DRAMATIC LESSONS
INCREASINGLY IMPORTANT
$750

LANGUAGE LESSONS
TWO A WEEK FOR TWO YEARS
$200

SIGHT READING
$100

IT CAN BE DONE
FOR $8,000
BUT FIGURE ON $9,550

Every year several thousand young people in the United States decide that they want to be opera stars.

They are eager, ambitious, intelligent, and they have good natural voices. Enthusiastic friends assure them that they sing beautifully, that they should have a career. They agree. They will be prima donnas, or leading tenors. They will rocket to success. They will "make" the Metropolitan, and thereafter lead the glamorous life.

Splendid! The Metropolitan does all that it can to help and encourage young American singers. Edward Johnson, general manager, believes that one of the important duties of the institution, and one upon which great stress should be placed, is its obligation to youthful artists. But he also believes that before a young person embarks on such a career, he should know just what he is facing. He should realize exactly what is involved in time, in money, in effort, in self-discipline and in sacrifice. For in the opinion of Mr. Johnson, character is as important as voice in the making of a great artist.

The Metropolitan is constantly besieged with requests for advice to beginners. Although it is impossible to give this individually, or to consider special problems, some general rules formed from the experiences of artists and teachers approved by the Metropolitan, give the prospective student an idea of requirements in both effort and expense.

The first rule is to select a teacher with a great deal of care. There are many excellent teachers of voice in America. The soundness of a teacher's method usually may be judged by the success of not one, but several, of his pupils, during a year's work. Serious damage may be done to a voice by improper training.

The student must be able to finance his period of preparation. In the opinion of some good teachers the average time required before a singer can expect financial return, is three years. The standard requirement is three lessons a week during the first year, and two a week for the first half of the second year. Then if the budget necessitates it, the number can be diminished, so that a lesson is taken only every other week during the last half of the third year.

Language lessons should be taken at the rate of two a week for at least two years. This includes instruction and practice in French, German and Italian.

Dramatic lessons should begin at the end of the second season of study and be continued for at least a year, complemented by dancing.

Sight reading should be studied for two to three years.

Study of piano is imperative.

During this three year period, if proper time is given to study, it is difficult to do other work. It is too soon to use the voice professionally, and there is rarely energy to spare for other employment. At the end of this time the properly taught student with a real voice is usually ready for the public. Various types of engagement are open in radio or church work, but the most valuable are those with secondary opera companies, where the young singer can gain experience in a variety of roles. It is only after a number of these have been completely mastered that he is ready to turn his thoughts toward a Metropolitan audition.

There has never been an operatic career of any length or importance which has not had as its foundation an apprenticeship of hard work and study. There was a time when study in Europe was almost compulsory for a grand opera career. With the constantly increasing number of good teachers in America, that is no longer true. But in addition to facilitating the study of languages, Europe occasionally offers a real advantage in its many opera companies with their opportunities for young artists. Once the voice is trained, the best school of grand opera is that of practical experience.

There have been operatic careers which have lasted the best part of a life time, and those which endured only a few brief seasons. The average length is about ten years. During this period the financial returns to a fine artist may be very great, though often from concert and radio rather than opera itself. A young artist frequently puts back into opera as much as is earned, in costumes, wigs, publicity and expenses attendant upon a career. A manager, an agent or publicity representative, a coach or accompanist are usually regarded as items of necessary expense in the budget of the successful opera singer. The demands upon a person in public life can be so great that even a large income becomes inadequate.

Nor does the need for effort cease with an operatic debut. Rather it increases. New roles must constantly be added to the repertory, old ones developed. The real artist accepts his responsibility. He feels that he must grow in a role, that it must be improved in interpretation and understanding every time he sings it. To this end he not only works and studies, but regulates his life, his entire regime having but one aim, the protection and development of his voice to its full possibility.

So the youthful singer, sighing for the glamorous life of an opera star, will do well to stop and consider. For the compensations of an operatic career are seldom luxury or ease. Glamour there is in plenty, but it is the glory of high idealism, hard work and genuine artistic accomplishment.

THE GLAMOROUS LIFE

An Opera Singer's Day

8:30	Breakfast
9:00	Breathing Exercises
9:30	Correspondence and Telephone
10:00	Vocalise
10:45	Taxi to Metropolitan
11:00	Rehearsal
1:00	Lunch
1:20	Costume Fitting
2:00	Conference with Manager
3:00	Home to study score
3:30	Practice with accompanist
4:00	Light dinner
5:00	Rest in bed
6:00	Hot bath and black coffee
6:45	Taxi to Metropolitan
7:00	Dressing room—make-up
7:20	Costume
7:30	Wig
8:00	The voice warm-up
8:40	On stage
11:08	Final Curtain
11:30	Light supper with friends
12:30	Bed

Metropolitan Tradition

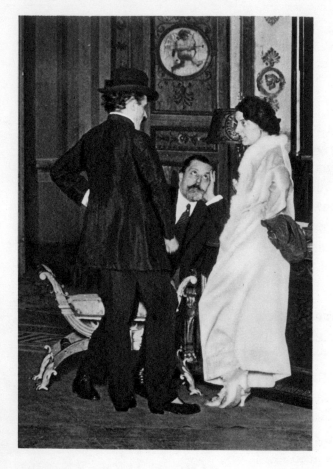

CONFERENCE—*The first "candid camera" picture in Metropolitan history. Arturo Toscanini, Giulio Gatti-Casazza and Geraldine Farrar discussing an important rehearsal problem on the Tosca set.*

ENRICO CARUSO, *a self-portrait*

THE METROPOLITAN.

Music . . . and memories.

For more than fifty years the mighty in the world of music have passed across its stage; famous voices have sounded constantly within its walls. For half a century it has been the musical shrine of America; for half a century it has been building a tradition, which places it among the great opera houses of the world. The old building is glorified by the splendor of its past. It is vibrant with the accumulated achievements of the years, which cast a spell over the vast auditorium, where in memory are blended the most beautiful voices of all time.

Even when the season is over, the red and gold is shrouded and the auditorium bare and deserted, the dream remains, a dream which goes back to an October evening in 1883, when the first Metropolitan Opening Night brought New York Society "uptown," curious and eager, to view the new Opera House, while the "Old Guard," scornful of the "great yellow brewery," remained loyally at the Academy of Music down in 14th Street.

There was reason for this loyalty. In thirty years the Academy of Music had become almost a family institution. From its stage Nilsson, Patti, Kellogg, Campanini, Lucca and Cary had won their way into Knickerbocker hearts. The manager, Colonel James Mapleson, gave New York the stars it loved.

But New York had grown, and new society not represented at the Academy of Music felt the need of a larger Opera House. They believed that New York would support a new and greater company. In line with this heresy they proposed the erection of the Metropolitan Opera House way up town at Broadway and 40th Street. It seemed a rash and pretentious undertaking, but the founders of the new institution were confident.

New York had been conscious of the interests of opera, both musically and socially, for seventy years. The war of 1812 was still vivid in memory when opera was first given in the old Park Theater in Park Row, and proved so popular that a new Opera House was erected in Astor Place, so that society might enjoy its music in a more suitable environment. In 1854, the town was deemed ready for another forward step, and the Academy of Music at the corner of Irving Place and 14th Street flung open its doors to an impressive audience, and the newspapers referred to the opening in the curiously modern terms "grand and gorgeous."

A generation later the opening of the Metropolitan eclipsed them all. Society came and sat in the boxes of the double gold horseshoe, to see and be seen under the light of an amazing gas chandelier. The most violent opposition was forced to admit the good points of the building, its dignity and restraint, the graceful curve of the galleries, the effectiveness of the Roman classic ornamentation, the artistry with which the figure of Apollo had been painted above the curtain opening. One enthusiast pointed out that "when this vast amphitheater was filled from parquet to roof, with an audience such as New York alone of all American cities could furnish, it constituted in itself a spectacle grander than any which could be put upon the stage."

However, an article in "The Critic," a literary magazine of the day, reflected another attitude with more than a touch of venom. It declared that "The opening of the Metropolitan Opera House on Monday evening seemed rather a social than a musical event. . . . We do not think the acoustic properties of the house are as good as those of the Academy of Music. . . . The voices had a muffled sound; and beyond the parquette chairs, or the horseshoe of boxes, one could not have enjoyed the performance though the performance had been enjoyable. None of the principals were in good voice, and Mme. Nilsson and Signor Campanini sang positively badly."

GUSTAV MAHLER

This fortunately was only one man's opinion. There were many more who thought Nilsson sang Marguerite in *Faust* like a veritable angel. At the conclusion of the performance she was called down from the lofty heights of Heaven to receive a golden wreath which due to the extraordinary feminine waistline of the day, it was pointed out, might also be used as a girdle. With Italo Campanini she responded to enthusiastic applause.

Manager Henry E. Abbey strove to make successive performances equally impressive. The casts he secured for the Metropolitan were a challenge which Col. Mapleson promptly accepted. It was a struggle to the death. When the smoke of battle cleared away it was the Metropolitan which endured, but with heavy losses and a changed management.

Seven years of opera in German, initiated by Dr. Leopold Damrosch thundered through the Metropolitan after that, the splendor of Wagner lightened by *Aïda*, *Don Giovanni* and *L'Africaine*. They were significant years, with the brilliant conductor Anton Seidl giving America its introduction to the *true* Bayreuth operatic tradition, and the first American performances of *The Ring*, *Tristan und Isolde and Meistersinger*.

But gradually Italian opera crept back into the repertory. Famous footsteps fell on an increasingly famous stage and the public hailed new stars with old favorites—a galaxy of names familiar even to a new generation of opera goers . . . names which laid solid foundations of Metropolitan tradition.

In 1892 a workman carelessly dropped a cigarette backstage and fire swept the building. When the Metropolitan Opera House was reopened in November, 1893, there was but one tier of parterre boxes, and from the sacred semi-circle which because of the jewelled display of its opening was immediately christened the Diamond Horseshoe, occupants surveyed an auditorium whose structure is virtually unchanged after four decades. Mr. Abbey was once more in charge. Later Maurice Grau joined him, to carry on alone after Mr. Abbey's death. Metropolitan tradition was growing. For abundance of sheer vocal talent this period has never been surpassed.

Triumph after triumph filled the great house with cheers and applause for his famous "ideal casts"—Nordica, Eames, Sembrich, Scotti, the great de Reszkés, Melba, Calvé, Gadski, Lilli Lehmann, Schumann-Heink, Pol Plançon, Bispham, Dippel, Lasalle . . . a host of magnificent artists whose memory has been a challenge in the world of opera ever since.

There was tragedy too. Death sat in the prompter's box—Armando Castelmary was stricken during a performance of *Marta*. Anton Seidl also died, and his funeral services were held on the stage of the Opera House he loved. There were pomp and circumstance in the famous gala performance for Prince Henry of Prussia, though the guest of honor tarried very briefly.

Sometimes there was unexpected comedy. Even the most devout Wagnerites were forced to laugh when during a performance of *Siegfried* the anvil proved obdurate, and the baffled tenor, Anthes, was forced to strike it again and again before it yielded. It was also Anthes who was singing *Lohengrin* when the Swan Boat collapsed during the triumphal entrance, and the hero was unceremoniously cast into the imaginary waters of a dusty back stage.

It was after the turn of the century that Grau's health failed and Heinrich Conried became general manager of the Metropolitan, bringing with him a splendid background of experience in the theatre, and injecting a new note into the purely musical atmosphere of the Opera House. Conried practically rebuilt the offices and installed new stage equipment, including the most modern version of that efficient contrivance, the trap door. With this installed it was possible for him to give the first American performance of *Parsifal*, over a storm of protest from the pious, on Christmas Eve of 1903. It was so successful that Conried repeated it eleven times that season.

It was Conried's new stage which upheld the feet of a nervous young tenor one night during the same year, when Enrico Caruso made his American debut in *Rigoletto*, achieving almost immediately a popularity which for sixteen years made a Caruso opening seem a command performance at the Metropolitan. On this stage Andreas Dippel appeared to rescue a performance of *Tannhäuser* substituting for Burgstaller at a few moments notice, And it was this stage on which fifteen soldiers fell when the bridge collapsed in the first act of *Carmen*.

The Metropolitan tradition grew as the seasons passed. The new floor boards were worn with exits and entrances. Tetrazzini, Homer, Bonci, Lina Cavalieri, Geraldine Farrar were added to the list of stars. Scotti established himself in the stellar position he retained for more than thirty years.

Conried, delighted with his initial successes, had other plans. Olive Fremstad thrilled and shocked New York as *Salome* in the premiere performance of the Strauss opera. *Hänsel und Gretel* was given for the first time at the Metropolitan with Humperdinck, the composer, coming from Europe to sit in the audience. Chaliapin launched his career. Gustav Mahler appeared for the first time in America to conduct *Tristan und Isolde*.

Conried's company lasted for five years and formed a link between the old style of opera in which voice was everything, and musical effect alone was significant, and the new, in which theatrical values took on importance.

In 1908, the Board of Directors announced that Giulio Gatti-Casazza, of La Scala, would become the next general manager of the Metropolitan. Andreas Dippel was appointed Administrative Manager.

Gatti arrived, inspected the Metropolitan Opera House, and announced plans for extensive changes. The first involved chorus and orchestra. Giulio

(Left, top to bottom) Nordica as Brünnhilde, Jean De Reszké as Raoul, Melba as Nedda, and Edouard De Reszké as Mephistopheles. (Above, right) An Opera Company Returns—Metropolitan singers after a tour which was ended by the destruction of San Francisco in 1906.

(Above, left to right) Tetrazzini as Violetta, Calvé as Carmen, Eames as Elsa, and Sembrich as Mimi.

ENRICO CARUSO in one of his greatest roles, Canio in Pagliacci. Caruso legends are never-ending but one he always enjoyed retelling concerned this same opera. A friend was singing Arlecchino, an off-stage part, and Caruso begged to be allowed to substitute in the role. He sang it superbly but no one in the audience of over 3000 people recognized the voice as better than that of the scheduled singer. This, Caruso delighted to say, proved that he was great only because of his reputation and not because of his voice!

Setti was brought from La Scala to direct the Italian voices. Arturo Toscanini, not quite so famous then, but already a great conductor, was engaged, and appeared on the podium to direct *Aïda* for a gala opening. Week after week names now famous dotted the program . . . Farrar, Cavalieri, Emmy Destinn, Fremstad, Alda, Alma Gluck, Gadski, Nordica, Amato, Rothier, Witherspoon, Slezak, Whitehill. There was a great farewell performance for Sembrich. Emma Eames said a quiet "Goodbye." Destinn, Caruso, Amato and Matzenauer sang at an opening performance of *Aïda* with Toscanini conducting, and more than 1000 persons were turned away. Tetrazzini appeared in *Lucia*, and Lucrezia Bori, who was to become an idol of the opera house, sang for the first time in *Manon Lescaut*. Martinelli made his debut in *La Bohème*. And still they came. Chaliapin, Braslau, Hempel, Mason, DeLuca, whose popularity never waned in seventeen years, John McCormack, Florence Easton, Charles Hackett, Reinald Werrenrath, Rosa Ponselle joined the distinguished company. Sophie Braslau appeared in *Boris*—Hempel in the premiere of *Der Rosenkavalier*.

In the early days Pavlova and Mordkin had spun dreams into reality. Other famous dancers floated across the Metropolitan stage—Isadora Duncan, Vera and Michael Fokine, Ruth Page, Adolph Bolm. Nijinski, a pale inspired being from another world, left a flashing eternal imprint of beauty. Rosina Galli made her debut as premiere ballerina in *Carmen*.

The development of recorded music broadened the interest in Opera. It had taken the voice of Caruso to the world, and the world paid tribute to him on the twenty-fifth anniversary of his operatic debut. Gifts were presented by Otto Kahn, President of the Board . . . a gold medal,—a silver vase from the chorus—a silver cup from the orchestra—and the flag of the city. That was a proud night for the Metropolitan. So was the Prince of Wales gala in 1919, with Alda, Easton, Ponselle and Caruso singing, and royalty sitting in a parterre box.

The seasons passed. Bodanzky had made his first appearance on the conductor's stand he was to grace so brilliantly for a quarter of a century. Caruso's voice as heard for the last time in *La Juive*. Maeterlinck and his wife sat in the audience for the premiere of *L'Oiseau Bleu*. Gigli and Chamlee made their debuts. Farrar sang *Zaza* and her youthful admirers were christened "Gerry Flappers" by W. J. Henderson, wit of New York music critics. Jeritza sang the aria in *Tosca* lying prone upon the stage, to the consternation of the conventional. Young artists climbed into public favor— Marion Telva, Queena Mario, Elisabeth Rethberg, Lauri Volpi, Tokatyan, and a fine young tenor known in Europe as Edoardo di Giovanni, who returned to America and the Metropolitan simply as Edward Johnson.

There was drama in the big theatre not included in the action of the opera. Marion Talley came out of Kansas, and her father sat at a telegraph key in her dressing room the night of her debut to flash the news of her rocketing success to the world. There were important events unrelated to music. The most successful Benefit ever held in the Opera House took place May 10, 1917, a testimonial to Marshall Joffre. The performance, one of the shortest in the history of the house, lasted from 9:30 to 10:45. Paderewski played and the chorus sang. The boxes, which sold for $1000 apiece, were oversubscribed by ten, and the performance brought in $92,238. More than $10,000 was donated by those who could not secure tickets, but forced their contributions to the French War Orphan Fund on the box office officials.

War time memories faded. Frederick Schorr and a young Dane by the name of Lauritz Melchior made their debuts, and with the matinee cycle of the *Ring*, German opera emerged from the doldrums. Dramatic ability took on new importance in opera. Pinza established himself as actor as well as singer. Grace Moore and Gladys Swarthout brought beauty and glamour. Lawrence Tibbett combined histrionic skill with a fine voice. Fresh from the provincial opera Casinos of France, Lily Pons found herself a great star.

As public interest broadened, a demand grew for opera in English. During his regime Gatti had produced a number of works by American composers. Among them were Walter Damrosch's *Cyrano*, Hadley's *Cleopatra's Night*, Taylor's *The King's Henchman*, Hanson's *Merry Mount*, Gruenberg's *Emperor Jones*. The most marked success was achieved by Deems Taylor's *Peter Ibbetson*. It opened the season of 1933, with Bori, Johnson and Tibbett in the leading roles.

By 1931 modern invention had laid violent hands on the dignity of the years. Radio invaded the sacred precincts, and from the Metropolitan stage the League of Composers sent a presentation of Stravinsky's *Oedipus Rex* over the air. The following Christmas the first opera performance was broadcast. The music which had been for so long confined to the old opera house, was at last going out to all America.

There were more new faces, new voices at the Metropolitan . . . Leider . . . Kappel . . . Ljungberg . . . Olszewska . . . Hofmann . . . Bonelli . . . Crooks . . . Lotte Lehmann . . . and at last the glorious Kirsten Flagstad. With a magnificent cast, headed by Flagstad and Melchior, Wagner became to the general amazement a "box office" attraction, and record-breaking crowds stormed the ticket window for admission. Their enthusiasm blotted out dark days, with their threat of disaster, when Bori's beloved voice pled from the stage to "Save Metropolitan Opera" and Geraldine Farrar came out of retirement to work for the continuation of the opera she loved. It was a strange, new day, but one toward which opera in America had been building for half a century — a day when opera began to be no longer a private luxury, but a public institution.

Gatti's departure in April, 1935, marked the end of an era. There was a gala performance in his honor, a last tearful farewell from the company as the S.S. Rex sailed away. Herbert Witherspoon, appointed to take his place, was formulating fine new plans for a reorganized opera when his activities were cut short by his untimely death. But the plans went forward . . . plans for a new and more modern opera.

On May 15, 1935, Edward Johnson was appointed manager of the Metropolitan Opera Company. One of the finest and best loved artists of the company, a tenor who had sung successfully for many years in Europe, and yet essentially a modern American, Mr. Johnson is able to view with equal sympathy the interests of management, artists and public. It has become his task to utilize the greatness of the past as a standard of measurement for the future. Out of fifty years of consecrated effort of great artists and great conductors, the Metropolitan legend has grown. The opera faces a new era, one of new demands from the public, new capacities in its singers. It must keep pace with the times. Whatever its development, the memory of its past must serve, not as a time dimmed recollection, but as a vital challenge to produce a future worthy of the great Metropolitan tradition.

19

FARRAR *as Madame Butterfly* (Top)
CHALIAPIN *as Boris*
AMELITA GALLI CURCI

Metropolitan Opera from Stage

Tonight at the Opera

TONIGHT you are going to the Metropolitan!

It is to be a gala evening, socially, musically and emotionally. The grand old house is already ablaze with lights, and the usual group of curious onlookers has gathered on the sidewalk outside the main entrance. All day there has been a patient line at the box office window, and long before curtain time the Broadway lobby is packed with people hoping for last minute tickets, or the possibility of buying standing room.

Perhaps you are in full evening dress for the occasion. From a strictly social standpoint, there is no time or place in America where formal dress is more clearly indicated than for a night at the opera. And there are those who feel that such preparation puts them in a more receptive mood for the evening's pleasure. The gowns and jewels of the women and the "white ties and tails" of the men add to the splendor of the scene. But this is true only of a certain section of the house; in others thousands of opera lovers appear in informal dress.

Subscribers usually enter through the Thirty-Ninth Street door. It is here that on opening nights and special occasions the glare of flash bulbs and the click of news cameras indicate the presence of the ever active society reporters for whom the Metropolitan has always been a happy hunting ground. But the taxi-riding audience generally arrives at the main entrance on Broadway where tickets are frequently offered on the sidewalk by the speculators the management tries so desperately to exclude. A favorite meeting place is under the bust of Caruso in the main lobby, or near the table where the essential Fred Rullman librettos of operas for the current week are sold, usually for thirty or fifty cents.

Hugh Brown, superintendent of the building, identified by his opera hat and welcoming smile, presides over the main door. Inside are two wide staircases, one on either side of the lobby, leading to the parterre boxes on the first landing, the grand tier and stall boxes on the second, and the dress circle on the third. Beyond, in the higher reaches of the house, are the balcony and the family circle.

Inside the main entrance, Al Irwin, the head usher, stands before the center door in a great semicircular foyer which extends half way around the auditorium. Following his directions, a member of a veteran staff, many of whom have been with the Metropolitan for twenty-five years, shows you to your seat.

The historic gold curtains are scheduled to part at seven thirty, eight or eight thirty, depending upon the opera. Unlike the theatre, the opera always starts promptly. Whether it is *Aïda* or *Tannhäuser*, *Trovatore* or *Bohème*, it will have its devotees, those who will be in their seats before the first down beat of the conductor's wand begins the overture, and who will not leave until the principals have bowed before the famous curtains for the

An evening at the Metropolitan is a gala occasion, and has been for over fifty-five years. Everyone feels it, from the smartly gowned box-holder to the last standee of the top gallery group which forms a semicircle just under the gold ceiling. Opera goers judge each performance individually: they all know that every night is a first night in opera.

last time, and the final echo of enthusiastic applause has died away. So you find yourself in good company, even though the house appears to be only half occupied. Only if you are a stranger will you note with surprise that the boxes fill quietly during the first act, and that the intermission proves the statement at the box office "House sold out."

In the little pause before the orchestra begins, you have a chance to look at the grandeur of the deep red and gold decoration, at the beauty of the proscenium arch, at the span of famous names above the stage, at the huge chandelier and rich upholstery of the comfortable new chairs which have replaced the antique seats with the persistent squeaks which were so long a feature of every Metropolitan season. You sense the atmosphere of this theatre, unique in America, unique indeed in the whole world. You think of the musical history which has been made here . . . the premieres . . . the revivals . . . the cheers and applause which have sounded in this auditorium. You think of the glamorous days when cabs rattled over cobblestones to deposit social leaders, resplendent with jeweled tiaras, stomachers, and the plumes and velvets of an era of magnificence. You think of the great artists . . . the great conductors . . . of all that has transpired within these walls. . . .

But now the orchestra, in the large pit before the stage, ceases tuning up. There is scattered applause as the conductor appears, makes his way through his men and mounts his stand. There is the rap of his baton, a moment of expectant silence, and the performance has begun.

Since the overture is in so many instances a vital part of the opera, late comers may cause you some annoyance. But though you are conscious that people are still making their way to the different parts of the house, you settle in your seat rejoicing over your promptness which enables you to enjoy every note.

And you think only of opera.

When the lights go up at intermission you look about at the audience, and wonder where all the people came from. You know that many of them are subscribers, people whose unflagging interest makes the opera season possible. Then there are those who can come only occasionally for some greatly anticipated performance, who have perhaps stood in line for hours on the day of the seat sale. There are the out of town visitors, some of them attracted by a genuine love of opera, some looking for celebrities, some of them simply "seeing the Metropolitan" as one of the main points of interest in New York. And last there is the large group of students and passionate music lovers, many of them of foreign birth,

WHAT THE OPERA AUDIENCE SPENDS

In order to attend sixteen weeks of opera, audiences at the Metropolitan Opera House spend nearly $400,000 for transportation, clothes, accessories, and between-the-acts snacks. Carefully checked surveys confirm the following conservative estimates:

EVENING DRESSES		$78,000
TAXICAB FARES		76,000
HOTELS AND TRANSPORTATION FOR OUT-OF-TOWNERS		63,000
RESTAURANT		50,000
OPERATION OF PRIVATE CARS		48,000
EVENING ACCESSORIES		40,000
FLOWERS		19,000
MEN'S EVENING CLOTHES		14,000

filling the upper galleries and usually making up the two large standee groups. The law allows four hundred standees.

If this is your first visit to the Metropolitan you will of course be curious about the famous Diamond Horseshoe—the parterre boxes which encircle the auditorium. These boxes have had tremendous significance in the history of the Opera House. A glance at your program will tell you that there are thirty-five of them, and their owners or tenants are easy to identify, since these names also appear in the program.

Among the upper tier of boxes you will recognize the large box at the left of the stage as that of the famous Opera Club. This group, founded in 1899, is sacred to men only, and enjoys its own club rooms across the foyer. Women are admitted as guests of members.

The character of a Metropolitan audience differs according to the day and the performance. Monday night is conceded by tradition to be society night, and there is usually a brilliant audience. Audiences for the *Ring* cycle are serious music lovers. A *Parsifal* performance becomes a sacred ceremony. Old favorites in the opera repertory often attract large out of town audiences, as does the appearance of a new or publicized star.

During the intermission there is always a dignified rush for the doors. You will want to visit the buffet and smoking room on the grand tier floor. Smoking in the corridors is strictly forbidden at the Metropolitan. For years it was limited to the cold lobbies or the overcrowded refreshment room. But recent improvements have provided an attractive lounge. Two rooms occupy the Broadway and down town side of the building to the extent of almost half a block. They are decorated artistically in blue and adorned with the portraits of opera stars of other days. The brilliantly lighted buffet, operated by Louis Sherry, has several hundred small tables. Red coated attendants spring to attention as the first comers appear in the doorway, and often serve more than one thousand persons swiftly and satisfactorily during the fifteen minute period before the warning bell announces the opening of the next act.

Since the exigencies of New York traffic cannot be denied, early leavers even more than late comers are likely to annoy the true opera enthusiast. With little respect for the death bed which is so traditionally the last act closing, they rustle determinedly up the aisle. The faithful remain to listen, spellbound, for the last notes to be sung; and as the orchestra fades into silence, the long applause and cries of "Bravo . . . Bravo" pay tribute to one more glorious performance in the famous old Metropolitan.

AS THOUSANDS CHEER—*Thousands acclaim Kirsten Flagstad and Lauritz Melchior for their history-making performances in* Tristan und Isolde. *Here they are acknowledging the deafening applause of a first-night audience.*

Masters
of Many Roles

Artists with repertory which includes a wide variety of roles are invaluable to an Opera House. A bass who takes in his stride Pogner, Méphistophélès and Fasolt, or a soprano who turns to the role of Flower Girl, Isolde or Gutrune with equal facility is dear to the Metropolitan heart. Substitution for a colleague in an emergency is one of the traditional courtesies of the opera. Historic examples are Manski's completion of Brünnhilde's appeal, to Wotan, for Leider when the latter's voice failed her, and Jagel's replacement of Martinelli, who was once stricken in the first act of *Aida*.

Among the artists noted for their extensive repertory are Brownlee, Bada, Cordon, Cehanovsky, D'Angelo, Doe, Jagel, Kaskas, Manski, Olheim, Petina, Pinza, Rothier and Votipka.

Dorothee Manski as Venus in Tann-häuser, Frederick Jagel as Gerald in Lakmé, Florence Easton in Jonny Spielt Auf. Below, Doris Doe as Annina in Rosenkavalier, Leon Rothier as the Commendatore in Don Giovanni, and clock mender Angelo Bada in L'Heure Espagnole.

On the opposite page is a set for Ernani by Urban.

METROPOLITAN PORTFOLIO

GÖTTERDÄMMERUNG, *Twilight of the Gods, is the final music drama in Richard Wagner's great saga of Norse mythology. This is the second act which records Gunther's return with Brünnhilde, rightful bride of Siegfried.*

DON GIOVANNI, originally known as The Reprobate Punished, was a success the first time it was produced, and has continued in favor for over 150 years. Mozart wrote the overture between midnight and morning on the day of this great opera's first performance.

Left, above, is Rosa Ponselle as Donna Anna and, below, Elisabeth Rethberg as Donna Elvira and Pavel Ludikar as Leporello. Above is Ezio Pinza as Don Giovanni.

The sextette, one of the best known of operatic selections, is the high point of the second act of Donizetti's Lucia di Lammermoor, which was based on the novel of Sir Walter Scott.

The Bazaar scene from act II of Lakmé.

The Bartered Bride, Smetana's gay opera now sung at the Metropolitan in English.

Marjorie Lawrence as Salome, at right. Below is Queena Mario as Gretel. Below, right, is Nino Martini making up for the role of Alfredo in La Traviata.

Edward Johnson as Pelléas. At right, Jan Kiepura, as the Duke in Rigoletto, Kerstin Thorborg as Fricka in Die Walküre, Paul Althouse as Walter in Die Meistersinger.

The quartette from La Bohème at left, with Adamo Didur as Colline, Pavel Ludikar as Schaunard, Beniamino Gigli as Rodolfo, and Antonio Scotti as Marcello. Below is a scene from Rimsky-Korsakoff's Coq d'Or with Lily Pons as the Queen of Chemakha whose fascination for King Dodon has just begun to work.

LUCREZIA BORI, the Grand Duchess of the Opera, a true artist, a beloved personality, a valiant crusader. Since her retirement from opera she has served as a member of the Board of Directors and has worked unceasingly for her great love, the Metropolitan.

Left, Bori in the garden scene from Don Pasquale.

Lawrence Tibbett appears at right in one of his greatest characterizations, Simon Boccanegra in the opera of that name. Above is Giovanni Martinelli in the title role of Otello, and Michael Bohnen (upper right) as Caspar in Der Freischütz. John Brownlee is below in Manon.

AÏDA, one of the most spectacular and most consistently popular of Verdi's operas, calls for a great many supers, some of whom are rehearsing at the right. What the mob scene is to the movies, supers are to the opera. Essential to the pageantry of operas such as Aïda, Coq d'Or, Samson and Carmen, supers march, stand, sit, or merely fill up the stage, half of them for the pay, half to be near great artists. Anywhere from one to three hundred may be required and are summoned by postcard. Once supers were mainly students who climbed around in the wings and generally got in the way; they were finally replaced by more conservative oldsters.

Senz, whose fame antedates that of Lon Chaney, is master of the Metropolitan's 3000 wigs and of make-up. No artist appears on the stage until Senz has given such final approval as he is bestowing here upon Elisabeth Rethberg. At the right the Rhine maidens are rehearsing for the scene of Das Rheingold in which they swim serenely in the depths of the great river, a tremendous temptation to the frustrated Nibelung Alberich.

Singing backstage, Editha Fleischer with piccolo accompaniment, gets the beat of the orchestra as relayed by an assistant conductor who watches the baton through a hole in the scenery.

THE WARM-UP — George Cehanovsky shows how, for nearly an hour before a performance, the artist warms up his voice while leisurely applying make-up for the first act. On a low note the vocal cords of a basso vibrate 75 times to the second, on a high note 300, a tenor 500, a contralto 650, a soprano about 1150. To start cold would strain them unduly.

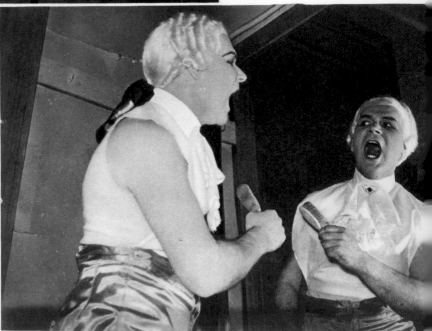

A SCENE FROM
BRUSCHINO

Emanuel List as Baron Ochs in
Rosenkavalier, one of the most
popular of the operas of Richard
Strauss, which was first produced
in New York in 1913. Revivals of
Rosenkavalier are enthusiastically
welcomed at the Metropolitan.

VERDI

RIGOLETTO
(above) The palace of
the Duke of Mantua
in Act I. Right is the
first act of Andrea
Chenier photographed
during the poet's aria.

ELEKTRA, which has
been revived with Rosa
Pauly. The public has
acclaimed, as enthusi-
astically as it once con-
demned, the short
Strauss masterpiece.

STRAUSS

In its quest for new operas, the Metropolitan has presented almost half a hundred novelties and revivals, of which twenty-two have been world premières. With perfect impartiality the great stage has been given over to the madness of Jonny Spielt Auf, the jungle chants of Emperor Jones, the underworld terrors of Merry Mount and the more facetious representation of the lower regions in Schwanda. Right, are scenes from Emperor Jones and Jonny Spielt Auf.

METROPOLITAN WORLD PREMIERES

	Seasons
The Pipe of Desire	1909-10
The Girl of the Golden West	1910-11
Koenigskinder	1910-11
Mona	1911-12
Cyrano de Bergerac	1912-13
Madeleine	1913-14
Madame Sans-Gêne	1914-15
Goyescas	1915-16
The Canterbury Pilgrims	1916-17
Shanewis	1917-18
The Dance in Place Congo (ballet)	1917-18
Il Tabarro Suor Angelica Gianni Schicchi	1918-19
The Legend The Temple Dancer	1918-19
L'Oiseau Bleu	1919-20
Cleopatra's Night	1919-20
Skyscrapers (ballet)	1925-26
The King's Henchman	1926-27
Peter Ibbetson	1930-31
The Emperor Jones	1932-33
Merry Mount	1933-34
In the Pasha's Garden	1934-35
The Man Without a Country	1937

41

THE FLYING DUTCHMAN, condemned in legend to sail the seas forever, is the subject of the music epic by Richard Wagner. Above is Friedrich Schorr as The Dutchman.

DIE MEISTERSINGER, Wagner's only humorous opera, is shown here in a rehearsal of Act II. Below is Herbert Witherspoon in the role of Pogner.

"WAGNER IS DEAD. LONG LIVE WAGNER!"

Today, due to the superb Wagner casts at the Metropolitan, he is gloriously alive and has a wider popularity in America than ever before. One of the greatest Isoldes in history is heard in Kirsten Flagstad, shown above in the first act of the opera. At the right is Karin Branzell.

43

Richard Crooks, who wears Caruso's own costume for the role Chevalier Des Grieux in Massenet's Manon. Below is Lotte Lehmann as the Feldmarschällin in Der Rosenkavalier and below, left, Giuseppe DeLuca as Lescaut in Manon.

Lily Pons as Lakmé. Tito Schipa as the Duke in Rigoletto and, below, Gladys Swarthout as Stefano in Romeo and Juliet.

Grace Moore in a scene with Lawrence Tibbett from The Tales of Hoffman, the last work of the French composer Offenbach.

SET FOR OTELLO by Donald Oenslager, a reproduction of the original drawing from which the set was designed.

SET FOR DIE WALKÜRE by Jonel Jorgulesco. Home of the Valkyries, from which the famous "Ho-jo-to-ho" is sung.

SIMON BOCCANEGRA, first presented by the Metropolitan in 1932, it became an outstanding success of the Season. Below are René Maison as Lohengrin, Mario Chamlee as Hans in The Bartered Bride, and Bidu Sayao as Violetta.

Strictly Business

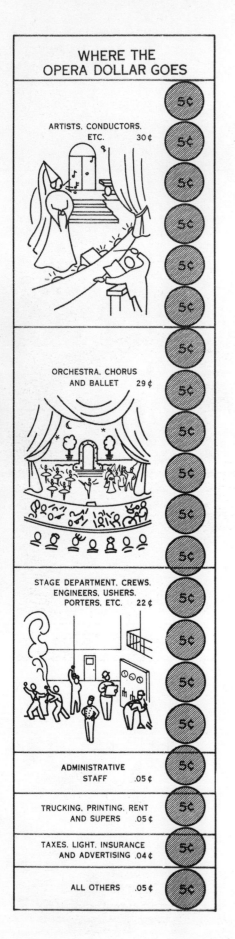

WHERE THE OPERA DOLLAR GOES

ARTISTS, CONDUCTORS, ETC. 30¢

ORCHESTRA, CHORUS AND BALLET 29¢

STAGE DEPARTMENT, CREWS, ENGINEERS, USHERS, PORTERS, ETC. 22¢

ADMINISTRATIVE STAFF .05¢

TRUCKING, PRINTING, RENT AND SUPERS .05¢

TAXES, LIGHT, INSURANCE AND ADVERTISING .04¢

ALL OTHERS .05¢

In the public mind the Metropolitan is a musical organization, not a commercial institution. But in spite of its educational and non-profit making nature, the most modern business practices must be applied to its management, which includes selection of the repertory, contracts with the individual artists and the various unions, the operation of the House departments, and the box office activities of subscription and ticket sale.

There have been various methods of management in the Opera House since the organization of the Metropolitan Opera-house Company, Ltd., in 1880. This company was incorporated with seventy stockholders to build a theatre where grand opera could be produced. The building was leased to Henry E. Abbey for the season 1883-1884 with disastrous financial results. For the next seven years the German Opera Company, first under the direction of Dr. Leopold Damrosch, and after his death that of Edmond Stanton, was sponsored by the stockholders. In 1891, Mr. Abbey returned in association with Maurice Grau to produce opera independently, but following the fire in August 1892, they announced that they would be unable to continue without a subsidy.

The demolished building was sold to the Metropolitan Opera and Real Estate Company, a corporation of thirty-five stockholders, each of whom reserved a parterre box for his use in lieu of rent. Of these new stockholders, about one-half had been members of the original company. Mr. Grau continued as manager until the 1902-1903 season, when the Metropolitan name was used for the first time for the operating company. Heinrich Conried, in order to lease the auditorium, was required to provide a $150,000 guarantee against loss, and in 1903 organized the Conried Metropolitan Opera Company with fourteen stockholders besides Conried, who owned about half of the stock. Conried was to share in the dividends and was paid a salary and given the proceeds of a special benefit performance.

The Metropolitan Opera Company came into existence in 1908 with the arrival of Mr. Gatti-Casazza as general manager. Otto Kahn, who had become increasingly active in the management, became chairman of the Board of Directors. The payment of dividends was discontinued, profits were to accumulate in a general fund for the security and improvement of the opera.

Since 1932, the Metropolitan Opera Association, Inc., has replaced the former Metropolitan Opera Company as the operating company. The Metropolitan Opera and Real Estate Company continues as owner of the House, the stockholders retaining their boxes and still providing the theatre rent free. During the times of financial stress it has been these stockholders who have been among the first to come forward with the assistance which has made the continuation of opera possible.

Present-day management of the Metropolitan lies in the hands of Edward Johnson, general manager, and two assistant managers, Edward Ziegler, and Earle R. Lewis, who serves also as box-office treasurer.

Mr. Johnson had long been a leading tenor of the Metropolitan, and before that a great favorite in the opera houses of Europe. He was known as a sound business man as well as a fine artist, and had the respect and affection of both artists and public. His appointment in 1935 was a very popular one, and inaugurated a new spirit at the Metropolitan. Mr. Ziegler has been assistant general manager since 1916. He was formerly music critic on *The New York Herald*, and combines musical erudition and practical experience. His long and whole-hearted devotion to the Metropolitan exemplifies the spirit of loyalty which permeates the entire organization. Mr. Lewis has presided over the Subscription Department at the Metropolitan for more than thirty years. He is a wizard at figures, can foretell the value of a season at a glance, and his promotional ability makes him the "Idea Man" of the Opera House. Frank Garlichs, who has been with the House for almost forty years, is treasurer of the Association.

The first duty of the management is the selection of the repertory, which must be made with careful consideration of public demand both for certain operas and casts. Popular operas must be distributed throughout the season, the same work must never be repeated in the same subscription series, and the Italian, German, French and American operas must be varied, all with proper consideration for the available artists and their schedules.

Artists' contracts are signed before the season opens and apply to roles, salaries, and number of appearances. They vary with the individual singers, some receiving a fee for each performance, some a weekly salary. The handling of the infinite detail connected with this department falls to Luigi Villa, Secretary to Mr. Johnson.

Metropolitan subscribers purchase tickets in books which admit them to a series of performances on the same day each week. Anyone may subscribe for tickets in any part of the House. Eight sets of tickets are constantly on sale during the season, the location indicated by color, and the performances indicated by number.

The Metropolitan income derives chiefly from subscriptions and sale of tickets, and from various gifts and donations. Its expenses include all operating costs and demand careful planning, with due consideration of the artistic standards involved. A balance of the two is Mr. Johnson's aim for a perfect Metropolitan budget.

EARLE R. LEWIS
and, *above*, EDWARD ZIEGLER

WHO RUNS
THE OPERA?

THE REAL ESTATE COMPANY
Provides the Building, Rent Free
Chairman of the Board, ROBERT S. BREWSTER

THE METROPOLITAN OPERA ASSOCIATION, INC.
Which Presents the Operas

President, PAUL D. CRAVATH
Chairman of the Board, CORNELIUS N. BLISS

THE MANAGEMENT
EDWARD JOHNSON   EDWARD ZIEGLER   EARLE R. LEWIS

DEPARTMENT CHIEFS

Treasurer	Musical Secy.	Secretary	Publicity	Advertising
FRANK GARLICHS	GIUSEPPE STURANI	LUIGI VILLA	FRANK WENKER	MARINO VILLA
Scenic Artist	*Master Mechanic*	*Chief Elec'n*	*Master of Properties*	*Construction Carpenter*
JOSEPH NOVAK	FRED HOSLI	JACOB BUCHTER	PHILIP CRISPANO	WILLIAM WARREN
Chief Engineer	*Technical Dept.*	*Costumer*	*Wigs & Make-up*	*Rehearsal Dept.*
FRANK KILKENNY	THOMAS HILLARY	N. L. LANZILOTTI	ADOLFH SENZ	JULES JUDELS

Supt. of Building, HUGH R. BROWN

SCOUTING FOR TALENT

Equal to the intense desire of every young singer to reach the Metropolitan is the ambition of the Metropolitan to secure the greatest artists available. It is popularly and erroneously believed that the Metropolitan sits austerely in its greatness and takes its pick of those who apply. Actually, with all the eagerness of the tyros waiting to be "discovered," the Metropolitan searches the musical centers of the world seeking both recognized artists and voices potentially great.

As the repertory of the company changes from year to year and the personnel alters, there must be replacements—new stars for important roles, new students for minor ones. They must be made carefully and with vision not only as to the singer's capabilities, but his relation to the company as a whole. Scouting for talent therefore becomes one of the major problems of the opera management.

A careful year round survey of the opera houses of Europe provides the basis for the annual quest for foreign artists. When Edward Johnson goes abroad each summer, he has the confidential reports of competent authorities regarding the possibilities in each country. In addition to his own "scouting" he must hear and judge those singers who have shown abilities as artists which seem to qualify them for the Metropolitan. With opera a part of the life of many cities in Europe, the number of singers is tremendous.

American artists who have the necessary qualifications are tested at stated intervals in the Opera House itself. Here on a bare stage, with piano accompaniment, the candidate faces the darkened auditorium where the General Manager and his assistant judges are listening. No decision may be made following a first hearing and several auditions are frequently required before a singer is engaged. Because the number accepted is necessarily so small in proportion to the number of candidates, the greatest care is exercised in making a choice.

The Metropolitan Auditions of the Air, sponsored by the Sherwin Williams Co., have become a vital factor in the development of opportunities for ambitious young American singers. Wilfred Pelletier, who is the head of the auditions committee, hears more than eight hundred of them annually. From this number it is necessary to select thirty-five who are heard on the air in the weekly broadcasts, and of these perhaps two or three may win the prize they most covet — a contract with the Metropolitan.

OPERA SINGERS' WORLD

Contrary to popular belief (and some foreign names assumed for stage purposes) there are more citizens from the United States among Metropolitan opera singers than from the rest of the world put together. In all, twenty of the world's sixty-odd countries are represented.

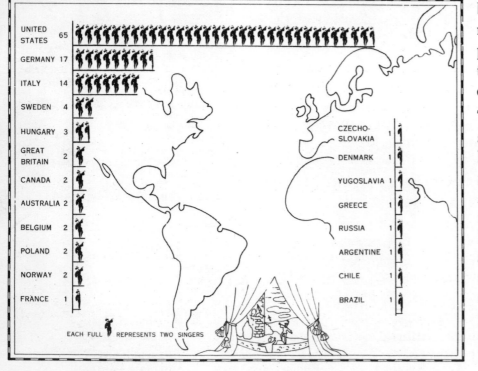

UNITED STATES	65
GERMANY	17
ITALY	14
SWEDEN	4
HUNGARY	3
GREAT BRITAIN	2
CANADA	2
AUSTRALIA	2
BELGIUM	2
POLAND	2
NORWAY	2
FRANCE	1
CZECHO-SLOVAKIA	1
DENMARK	1
YUGOSLAVIA	1
GREECE	1
RUSSIA	1
ARGENTINE	1
CHILE	1
BRAZIL	1

EACH FULL REPRESENTS TWO SINGERS

CONTROL BOARD—*Playing on an instrument peculiarly like an organ, Adolph Werber sits beside the prompter and runs off the lighting cues from master electrician Buchter's "score." Under the stage are 176 radio-like reactors connected by this master board, through which the effects are produced. Fire, moonlight, rippling water and clouds are secured by skillful lighting which must be timed as precisely as an entrance cue.*

WHEN THE CURTAIN FALLS

There are those who prefer to know nothing of operations back stage, who feel that to understand the mechanics deprives a production of its glamour. But for most people the dim area of the wings holds endless fascination. There is no department of opera which runs with greater efficiency than the stage crew.

During the season the Metropolitan gives five subscription performances a week, a popular priced series on Saturday evening and a concert on Sunday. There are out of town performances on Tuesday nights, and a number of special matinees. Frequently as many as ten different productions must be staged within seven days. Since all of the scenery used at the Opera House is kept in warehouses throughout the city and must be brought to the theatre for each performance, the activities of the backstage crew become of major importance. There must be the utmost speed, accuracy and attention to infinite detail.

Head of the Stage Department is Frederick Hosli, who directs a crew of forty-five men. They include six carpenters, nine storehouse men, nineteen regular stage hands, and eleven who make up the special night crew. During the performance they stack each set at the end of the scene and store it at the back of the stage near the great Seventh Avenue entrance. When the final curtain falls, and the order "Strike the set" is given, nothing remains but to add the last scene to the accumulated load and start it for the warehouse.

The scenery for each opera is stored in a unit, and so arranged that it may be withdrawn on a few hours' notice. The same truck which takes the set to the storeroom brings back the one for the succeeding performance. It is loaded into the Opera House, and left for the stage crew to set up on the following day. The actual setting up of the stage is done according to blue prints which are posted for each performance. The stage is chalked off and each piece put into exact position. For some of the operas there are floor cloths which indicate the position of the furniture, but in the majority of cases the stage is freshly marked each time. Some scenes are exceedingly difficult to put up. The first act of *Tristan*, for example, has 2000 separate pieces that take nearly five hours to bolt together.

Between scenes the work takes place with clock-like precision, the Master Mechanic timing every move, so that intermissions may be scheduled exactly. The work is highly departmentalized. Carpenters, repair men, and electricians have their definite assignments. Each must operate with the interlocking precision of wheels in a fine watch. Then and only then can a production move smoothly to its grand finale.

PROPS—*The horse in Götterdämmerung, the donkey in Pagliacci, the pony in Mignon, the frankfurter in Meistersinger, the chandelier in Traviata, all are props, as is everything that goes on the stage except the scenery and the artists. The Metropolitan has over 25,000 props, many in duplicate, and all listed in Philip Crispano's notebook, a page from which is reproduced below. Lost props are a rarity, occasionally one is filched by a sentimental super.*

```
     " M A G I C   F L U T E "
            P R O P S

ACT I:

 Bow
 Snake
 3 Silver Spears
 1 Forest Flute (5 Notes in tune)
(1 Bird cage with birds (made of
       willow)
(1 Bird cage (later, the same with-
       out birds
 Jug for water
 1 Stone
 1 Strong lock
 1 Medallion with picture and
       chain
 1 Bunch of lilies for Queen
 1 Golden Flute (with string)

ACT II:

 Couch with cushions
 4 Hand chains (for Slaves)
 2 Daggers
 3 Silver palm branches (for
       Genien)
 Elephant with throne and Bald-
    achin, ladder for dismounting
 4 Spears with tassels
 2 Fans for colored slaves
 1 King  (stick) for Sarasto
 About 10 sticks (for Nobles)
  "     4 sticks for Court
       ladies, with ribbons and
       flowers, golden leaves
```

Fiddlers'

Tristan und Isolde reaches its glorious climax. Wave upon wave, the music which seems as eternal as the love it describes mounts to its final ecstasy and is hushed into silence. As the applause thunders, the ninety-three musicians who for hours have been weaving the spell of sound take their instruments and make their way through the little doorway which leads into "Fiddlers' Alley."

"Fiddlers' Alley" is the name given to the section of the Opera House directly under the stage which is dedicated to the use of the men in the orchestra. But there is no lingering here after a performance. As long and as taxing as is the *Tristan* score, such an opera is but one of eight or nine performances which make up the weekly routine of the Metropolitan orchestra. So the musicians are off to snatch a few hours' sleep before rehearsal time in the morning.

The Metropolitan maintains a basic orchestra of ninety men, with a reserve from which are called additional players for the stage band, or to augment the men in the pit for special performances. Members of the orchestra must not only be excellent musicians, but familiar with the entire opera repertory, and able to make the adjustments required by a change of conductors for each performance. Many of them have played with ranking symphony orchestras, and have reputations as soloists. They are selected and reauditioned from season to season by means of a "blindfold test," each man playing required selections from behind a screen, so that his identity is unknown to the judges.

In addition to the performances each evening, and the several matinees, rehearsals are constant. They begin two and a half weeks before the opening of the season, and continue each morning with the exception of matinee days.

The orchestra pit at the Metropolitan is one of the largest in the United States. Most of the musicians are seated in pairs, each couple reading from a copy of his own part of the score. These copies are prepared and sent down in advance of each performance from the Metropolitan's own extensive music library. Under the stage the orchestra has private quarters where there are lockers for street clothes and instruments, and a recreation room where the men may smoke and relax between acts.

It is the conductor who is often the unknown hero of the opera. Faces and personalities of principals, chorus members and ballet become familiar

Top, Artur Bodanzky, one of the world's most brilliant conductors of German opera. Below are an offstage serenade in Louise, an orchestra rehearsal, and a stage orchestra costumed for the fête in Don Giovanni.

Alley

to the opera-goer, but the conductor is known only through his interpretation. He is a force rather than an individual, a dark shadow outlined against the glare of the stage. Campanini, Leopold and Walter Damrosch, Seidl, Mancinelli, Schalk, Hertz, Mottl, Mahler, Toscanini, Polacco, Serafin, Panizza and Bodanzky are among the Metropolitan's famous silhouettes.

The conductor's stand is directly in the center, elevated above the orchestra pit to bring the conductor's head and shoulders in line with the vision of the performers. Many people think the conductor is responsible only for leading the orchestra. Actually he must coordinate the entire production. Every beat of his baton must be followed by the singers as well as the orchestra. Even the prompter who stands in a hooded pit in the footlights follows the baton in a mirror. It is the conductor who indicates every cue and sets the pace. Most conductors have strong theories regarding vocal as well as orchestral interpretation, and the manner in which they must be combined into a finished performance. A conductor's background must include thorough understanding of the possibilities of the score he is conducting. It is his scholarly, sensitive interpretation which must animate the performance.

The actual conducting of a performance of any opera is the culmination of months of work on the part of the conductor, and the coordination of the efforts of many persons. Long before the scheduled performance Mr. Johnson, with the conductor and Giuseppe Sturani, the musical secretary, has selected the cast; and principals, orchestra and chorus have been at work on their respective parts. First rehearsals with piano are called for the principals by an assistant conductor, and orchestra and chorus are rehearsed separately. The conductor then takes charge and there are ensemble rehearsals with piano, and then two or three rehearsals with orchestra before the general or dress rehearsal.

During a performance, the prompters and assistant conductors direct chorus groups in the wings and give the principals their cues, working in absolute accord with the conductor. This is imperative, for the conductor must shoulder the final responsibility for the performance, however many vocal deficiencies may occur, or temperamental artists defy his authority.

A resourceful technician, an authority on voice, an imaginative director with a dramatic concept of the possibilities of the music, a man of tact, authority and understanding, an inspired leader—such a man may be a Metropolitan conductor, provided he has "The score in his head, not his head in the score."

METROPOLITAN CONDUCTORS
Ettore Panizza (top) Wilfred Pelletier, Gennaro Papi, and Erich Leinsdorf.

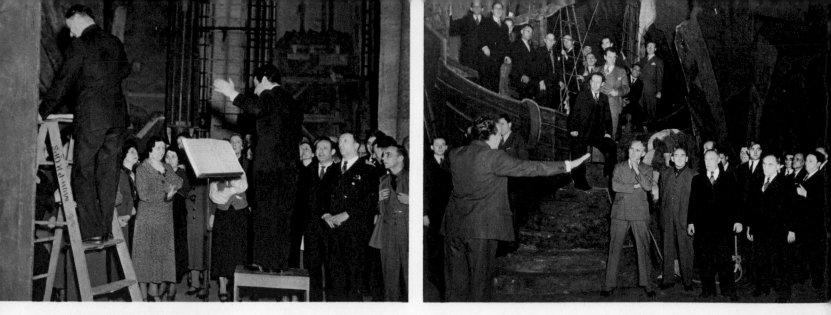

The chorus singing off-stage, coordinated with the orchestra by the assistant conductor on the ladder. Right is a chorus rehearsal for The Flying Dutchman.

THE CHORUS

CHORUS VETERAN — *Maria Savage, with the Metropolitan for over thirty years, saw her daughter make her debut as a chorister fourteen years ago.*

The Metropolitan chorus is a miniature League of Nations, with ninety-four members. Americans, British, Belgians, Frenchmen, Germans, Italians, Russians, and Scandinavians—they sing some seven performances a week in any one of four languages, and play cards together between scenes.

Getting into the chorus is not easy and the choristers live in a little world all their own. Ability as to sight-reading, repertory, stage business and languages must be established before entrance, and every member is auditioned annually. Many of the choristers know from sixty to eighty roles! There are no divisions as to language, and the entire chorus always sings as a unit. The fifty men and forty-four women are rehearsed separately by Chorus Masters Fausto Cleva and Konrad Neuger, and the ensemble is then taken over by the director and conductor. Rehearsals average three hours daily.

Before a performance members of the chorus go to their special dressing rooms, where each has an assigned place at a long make-up table. They get into costume and wait for a signal bell to summon them. If the chorus is off-stage, as it frequently is, an assistant conductor climbs a ladder and gives the beat by following the conductor in the pit. The group fills the wings, but moves in an orderly formation with almost military precision.

Most chorus members have excellent voices and make their work in the chorus a life-long profession. Twenty-five years of service is no unusual record at the Metropolitan. In fact, age became a point of criticism from the public, and the management, yielding to the argument that laughing village lasses should look the part, has made some changes. But there are excellent character actors in this group whose bits of pantomime give an air of reality to the performance. Though their faces and figures have grown so familiar to the habitual opera-goer that chorus members sometimes seem a little too much like old friends in fancy dress, the adaptability with which members of the group transform themselves from the scrappy cigarette girls in *Carmen* to ladies-in-waiting in *Aïda*, from simple villages in *Faust* to the clowning apprentices of *Die Meistersinger* is nothing short of miraculous. Few indeed are the operas without a chorus. Even Wagner, Who ignored it completely in *Rheingold*, *Walküre* and *Siegfried* used choristers in *Lohengrin*, *Tannhäuser*, *Götterdämmerung* and *Parsifal*.

Occasionally a chorister graduates to an artist's role, but this is rare. Minnie Egener, who sang many secondary roles at the Metropolitan, was an exception. Mario Laurenti was another. Claudia Muzio, whose father and mother were both choristers, and who was a true "baby" of the opera, made her debut on the stage across which she had often toddled as a child. But for the most part a chorister remains a chorister, proud of his place in a group which contributes so much to the richness and beauty of opera.

BORIS ROMANOFF

THE BALLET

With the engagement of Boris Romanoff as Choreographer and Ballet Master, the Metropolitan is developing its own ballet as part of the opera ensemble, not merely to give color and life to the production, but to emphasize the artistic value of the ballet in its own right.

The ballet has always been recognized as a part of opera, usually occupying a fixed place in the performance. Indeed there is the historical instance of the reaction of a Paris audience against the initial performance of *Tannhäuser* because the ballet was in the first act instead of the second, where custom dictated that it belonged. But that same custom has often included a ballet because the opera called for one, with not too much emphasis on its individual character. Nevertheless it has brought great dancers to the Metropolitan. Pavlova and Mordkin have become a tradition; Rosina Galli, Adolph Bolm, Rita de Leporte, Ruth Page, Bonfiglio have made their contributions. For years Miss Galli directed the ballet performances. After her departure the American Ballet introduced a distinctly modern note, but operated as a unit separate from the Metropolitan. Under the new plan the ballet has once more become an integral part of Metropolitan Opera activity.

Boris Romanoff studied at the Imperial Ballet School in St. Petersburg, was at one time a disciple of Fokine, and later became premier danseur for the Diaghileff Ballet Russe. He was Ballet Master and dancer for Pavlova. For four years he has been associated with the Royal Theater of Rome as Ballet Master and Choreographer. At the Metropolitan he is building his own ballet and the roof stage once more vibrates with the pat-pat of toe slippers as through endless rehearsals the various routines go forward toward perfection. The ballet school, directed by Miss Margaret Curtis, will be continued to provide instruction for youngsters willing to undergo the strenuous routine which may one day make them candidates for the Metropolitan stage. It is from this school that juvenile groups required in various operas are recruited.

THE BALLET SCHOOL

OPERA
REPERTORY

Successful presentation of grand opera is always dependent upon the capacity of the artists available to interpret it. There must be a bass baritone adequate to the demands of *Don Giovanni*, a baritone who can toss off the impudent "Figaro, Figaro" of *The Barber of Seville* a soprano who can carry the heavy dramatic burden of *Tosca*. In some seasons an extraordinary cast, or the outstanding interpretation of a leading role swings the pendulum of public favor, and brings German, Italian or French opera, as the case may be, into spectacular popularity. The discovery of a Lily Pons calls for a revival of *Lucia di Lammermoor*, *Lakmé* and other operas suited to the display of her coloratura talents. A Caruso brings Italian opera into ascendency. A Flagstad and a Melchior inspire intense enthusiasm over the great music dramas of Wagner.

The Metropolitan meets the demand for such performances by scheduling the maximum number which may be given in a balanced season. It is proverbial that the opera novice often comes at first to hear an individual artist, and through this initial enthusiasm learns to love opera for its own sake. But the Opera House has no star system and makes no distinction between its casts, believing that the production as a whole is of more importance than the individual performance. The ideal of the management is to keep French, German and Italian opera in proper relation, and maintain a balanced repertory at all times.

This is no simple task. Opera-goers have wide diversity of taste. Standard productions and old favorites must be interspersed with revivals and novelties, and there is a never-ending search for opera in English. Sympathetic to the freshness and vigor of modern composition, and eager to foster it whenever possible, the Metropolitan also regards as its duty the presentation of masterpieces of the past to a new generation. As a great art museum treasures its master paintings, paintings done with technique unknown to the present day artist with modern concepts, so the Metropolitan guards the traditional presentations of opera as the heritage of a generation which otherwise might never know them. Consideration of this obligation is one of many factors guiding the selection of the repertory.

Although it varies somewhat from year to year, the repertory of the Metropolitan usually includes in Italian, the following operas: DONIZETTI: *Lucia di Lammermoor*; LEONCAVALLO: *Pagliacci*; MASCAGNI: *Cavalleria Rusticana*; MOZART: *Don Giovanni*; PONCHIELLI: *La Gioconda*; PUCCINI: *Gianni Schicchi, La Bohème, Madama Butterfly, Tosca*; ROSSINI: *Il Barbiere di Siviglia*; VERDI: *Aida, Il Trovatore, La Forza del Destino, La Traviata, Otello, Rigoletto, Simon Boccanegra*.

Among the German operas are: BEETHOVEN: *Fidelio*; HUMPERDINCK: *Hänsel und Gretel*; STRAUSS: *Der Rosenkavalier, Elektra, Salome*; WAGNER: *Der Fliegende Holländer, Die Meistersinger, Die Walküre, Götterdämmerung, Lohengrin, Parsifal, Rheingold, Siegfried, Tannhäuser, Tristan und Isolde*.

The French group includes: BIZET: *Carmen*; DELIBES: *Lakmé*; GOUNOD: *Faust, Roméo et Juliette*; HALÉVY: *La Juive*; MASSENET: *Manon*; OFFENBACH: *Les Contes d'Hoffmann*; RIMSKY-KORSAKOFF: *Le Coq d'Or*; SAINT-SAËNS: *Samson et Dalila*; THOMAS: *Mignon*.

Opera in English, translated or otherwise, has recently been represented by TAYLOR: *Peter Ibbetson*; SMETANA: *The Bartered Bride*; DAMROSCH: *The Man Without a Country*; MENOTTI: *Amelia Goes to the Ball*.

THE OPERA GUILD

OLGA SAMAROFF STOKOWSKI

director of the Guild's opera courses which are open to the public.

A GUILD PARTY — *Below, with Lawrence Gilman, Mrs. August Belmont, Lawrence Tibbett, Mrs. Walter Sands Marvin, Lauritz Melchior and Mrs. Herbert Witherspoon.*

Opera lovers are found today far beyond the traditional frontiers of Fifth Avenue and Park—far beyond the confines of New York itself. They may be discovered in every city in the country, in every town and hamlet. They include the subscribers who are the backbone of opera. They also include those who perhaps have never seen the Opera House at all but share the ardent enthusiasm for opera which is typical of the most devoted of Metropolitan audiences.

It was to find and fuse this great opera public that Mrs. August Belmont founded the Metropolitan Opera Guild in 1935. The purpose of the Guild was to promote intelligent understanding of opera—Metropolitan Opera. Thanks to an able Board of men and women, within a few months several thousand Guild members were actively assisting. Soon the membership doubled. It has gone on steadily increasing.

Today Metropolitan Opera Guild influence extends throughout the world with long distance memberships in Alaska, South Africa and the Hawaiian Islands. Branches have been established in Philadelphia and San Francisco. Operagrams, the Guild's annual publication which originated as a brief primer, has become an inclusive manual of plots and biographies, with guides which enable radio listeners to visualize the characters on stage at any point in the performance, and lists of recordings and reference books. The Opera News is sent weekly during the season to the entire membership and tells the story of intimate backstage happenings, of new artists and the significance of unusual works. Today, at the invitation of The National Broadcasting Company, the Guild has a radio hour, a weekly coast-to-coast broadcast on opera over the N. B. C. network. The opera of the week—the Saturday broadcast—is discussed and its chief themes played by a musical ensemble.

To its members near New York, the Guild has brought unique privileges. The first is an opportunity to attend a rehearsal of one of the unusual operas in the Metropolitan repertory. The second is an invitation to a gala evening at which new members of the opera company are often presented.

The management looks to the Guild to determine the preferences of its membership. Following the members' expressed choice, such works as *Der Rosenkavalier*, *Le Coq d'Or* and *Boris Godunoff* have reappeared on the prospectus. The educational work of the Guild is one of its most important activities. As a first step, the Guild established a fund to provide opera tickets at prices within the reach of

Young Opera-goers – a Guild Junior Audience.

music students, and contributions were received commemorating Scotti, Schumann-Heink and Farrar. The Guild found a tremendous interest in opera among young people and, as an experiment, a performance of Aïda was offered to school children by the Guild at prices from $.25 to $2.00. So successful was this performance and so widely was it praised that the following season children came from more than fifty communities for two performances of the *Barber of Seville*. Now *Lohengrin* and *Otello* have been added to the calendar and schools in Westchester, New Jersey and New York send huge delegations to these special performances.

Urgent requests for information on opera led the Guild to sponsor public lectures on the *Ring* and *Der Rosenkavalier*. These have grown into a public "Layman's Opera Course" conducted by Olga Samaroff Stokowski.

The Guild has materially aided the Opera House by providing, at Mr. Johnson's request, a huge cyclorama through which the realistic production of many operas has been greatly enhanced. The musician's room has been modernized and a collection of portraits of famous opera stars of the past has been assembled in the Lounge.

Guild member Charles D. Jackson escorts Honorary Guild Chairman Lucrezia Bori to a board meeting.

With an eye to the future of the Metropolitan, the Guild has laid the foundation for an Endowment Fund, and a reserve for special emergencies which serves as a nucleus for additional legacies and gifts. More than $33,000 has already been contributed. Further large sums have passed through the Guild treasury to the Metropolitan in the form of subscriptions and ticket sales, cleared through the Guild's ticket secretary as an additional service to city members.

At the Guild's headquarters, 654 Madison Avenue, New York City, an active staff under the direction of Mrs. Herbert Witherspoon, with Mrs. John DeWitt Peltz as director of publications, serves the growing membership, and furnishes information to anyone desiring to join its ranks.

Since Mr. Johnson's first welcome to the Guild as "an integral part of The Metropolitan Opera Association," it has endeavored to act as liaison between opera and public. Today its members welcome the responsibility of further interpretation and service to those who seek to know more of opera. From the reaches of the air, from the fresh company of youth, flock the new audience for opera. The Guild is proud to bind them into a strong support for the unique national institution that is the Metropolitan.

OPERA
ON THE AIR

On Christmas afternoon in 1931 the Metropolitan Opera Company and the National Broadcasting Company joined together in giving a significant Christmas present to the world, the first broadcast performance of grand opera in America.

The gift was so gratefully received that they have since continued to play the role of Santa Claus with a series of Saturday afternoon performances which have given millions of listeners their first opportunity to understand and enjoy the lyric theater. Opera which was once a private luxury, has become a public possession. Eighty stations in the United States and Canada, and short wave transmission all over the world, make its enjoyment universal.

Fan letters on the opera broadcasts reveal a cross section of American life. Women's groups, study clubs, schools, and colleges, housewives, workingmen in shops and camps, lonely persons in remote places, opera lovers and those to whom opera is a curiosity, every class and strata of society make up the listening group and now demand their favorite stars and their favorite repertory, and write of their likes and dislikes definitely and with critical authority.

The skill with which the opera is broadcast seems to be of as much importance as whether it is broadcast at all. Box 44 in the grand tier at the Metropolitan, where each Saturday the technical apparatus is installed, is a center of interest to thousands. Here the microphones which pick up voices and orchestra are connected to a central tone control board designed and operated by Charles C. Grey, engineer in charge of Metropolitan Opera broadcasts. Eight microphones are used. Four are suspended above the orchestra; the other four are in the footlights, placed in pairs of close and long perspective microphones, the former for nearby voices, the latter for those further away. As the artists move about the stage, the engineer must adjust these microphones through the control board and blend the various tones so that the listener hears the same musical quality he would hear if he were sitting in Box 44.

Mr. Grey sits in semi-darkness, his eyes on the stage while his hands automatically control the mixer. Behind him in the box is a score reader who warns him of approaching climax. Beyond a glass door at the rear of the box are an assistant engineer and Milton Cross, the announcer, with his own microphone. He not only describes the audience and the cast, but gives a clear outline of the action in each scene.

The broadcasts of grand opera are a splendid technical and artistic achievement. They are proof of the advance of American invention and eloquent testimony to the spread throughout America of appreciation of great music.

MILTON CROSS
opera commentator.

Within the reach of every radio set in the United States (and nearly every set in the world), the broadcasts of the Metropolitan Opera by the National Broadcasting Company are heard by millions of eager listeners each week. In special listening groups, opera "clubs" and in private homes, these great performances make an everlasting impression on young and old alike.

BOX 44 – from which the radio broadcasts of Metropolitan Opera are controlled. In the cloak room at the back of the box Mr. Cross describes the opera.

SUCCESS STORY

In addition to bringing the Metropolitan to the world, the radio brings singers to the Metropolitan. Each year the Opera Auditions of the Air give scores of talented young artists an opportunity to demonstrate their ability and win, if they can, a place in the opera company. Here Lucielle Browning, audition winner from North Carolina, is signing the much coveted contract with Edward Johnson.

AN OPERA COMPANY

Even though it may vary but slightly from year to year, to assemble an opera company is a gigantic task. There must be a balance of voices and a group of directors, chorus masters and conductors, technically and artistically equipped to cast and rehearse individual talents into a mold for an opera. Here is the present Metropolitan company:

SOPRANOS

LINA AIMARO	PHILINE FALCO	MARJORIE LAWRENCE	LILY PONS
JOSEPHINE ANTOINE	MARITA FARELL	LOTTE LEHMANN	ELISABETH RETHBERG
ROSE BAMPTON	MAFALDA FAVERO	DOROTHEE MANSKI	BIDU SAYAO
PEARL BESUNER	SUSANNE FISHER	QUEENA MARIO	MAXINE STELLMAN
NATALIE BODANYA	KIRSTEN FLAGSTAD	ZINKA MILANOV	GRETE STÜCKGOLD
VINA BOVY	DUSOLINA GIANNINI	GRACE MOORE	CHARLOTTE SYMONS
HILDA BURKE	MARGARET HALSTEAD	MARISA MOREL	ROSA TENTONI
MARIA CANIGLIA	HELEN JEPSON	EIDE NORENA	THELMA VOTIPKA
MURIEL DICKSON	IRENE JESSNER	ROSE PAULY	

MEZZO-SOPRANOS AND CONTRALTOS

KARIN BRANZELL	DORIS DOE	HELEN OLHEIM	GLADYS SWARTHOUT
LUCIELLE BROWNING	ANNA KASKAS	IRRA PETINA	ENID SZANTHO
BRUNA CASTAGNA	KATHRYN MEISLE	RISË STEVENS	KERSTIN THORBORG
			GERTRUD WETTERGREN

TENORS

MAX ALTGLASS	RICHARD CROOKS	CHARLES KULLMANN	NICHOLAS MASSUE
PAUL ALTHOUSE	ALESSIO DE PAOLIS	KARL LAUFKOETTER	LAURITZ MELCHIOR
JUSSI BJOERLING	CHARLES HACKETT	RENE MAISON	GIORDANO PALTRINIERI
ARTHUR CARRON	CARL HARTMANN	GIOVANNI MARTINELLI	GEORGE RASELY
JOHN CARTER	FREDERICK JAGEL	NINO MARTINI	SYDNEY RAYNER
MARIO CHAMLEE	JAN KIEPURA	GALLIANO MASINI	ARMAND TOKATYAN
			ERICH WITTE

BARITONES

RICHARD BONELLI	DONALD DICKSON	HERBERT JANSSEN	JOHN CHARLES THOMAS
JOHN BROWNLEE	WILFRED ENGELMAN	CARLO MORELLI	LAWRENCE TIBBETT
GEORGE CEHANOVSKY	ARNOLD GABOR	HANS HERMANN NISSEN	LEONARD WARREN
LOUIS D'ANGELO	DANIEL HARRIS	FRIEDRICH SCHORR	ROBERT WEEDE
	JULIUS HUEHN	CARLO TAGLIABUE	

BASSOS

HERBERT ALSEN	VIRGILIO LAZZARI	NICOLA MOSCONA	ADOLF VOGEL
NORMAN CORDON	EMANUEL LIST	EZIO PINZA	JAMES WOLFE
JOHN GURNEY	POMPILIO MALATESTA	LEON ROTHIER	

CONDUCTORS

ARTUR BODANZKY	ERICH LEINSDORF	GENNARO PAPI	KARL RIEDEL
	ETTORE PANIZZA	WILFRED PELLETIER	

ASSISTANT CONDUCTORS

OTELLO CERONI	RICCARDO DELLERA	KARL RIEDEL	FREDERICK VAJDA
PIETRO CIMARA	ANTONIO DELL'OREFICE	GIACOMO SPADONI	HERMANN WEIGERT
FAUSTO CLEVA	EDOARDO PETRI	VITTORIO TRUCCO	FELIX WOLFES

CHORUS MASTERS

FAUSTO CLEVA   KONRAD NEUGER

STAGE DIRECTORS

DESIRE DEFRERE   HERBERT GRAF   LEOPOLD SACHSE

BALLET MASTER AND CHOREOGRAPHER

BORIS ROMANOFF

LIBRARIAN

ALFRED MAPLESON

METROPOLITAN ON SAFARI

With a special freight train all its own and a string of ten Pullman cars, every year in spring the Metropolitan goes on safari. The trek begins from New York with principals, chorus and orchestra practically taking over one of the city's railroad terminals, and ends its first march in Baltimore, going from there to Boston for ten days of packed houses. Then the company moves on to Cleveland where in the great convention hall congregate one of the largest operatic audiences in the world: 68,000 in seven days. The next stop is Rochester, and then the company returns to New York for special Holy Week performances.

Once the trip extended as far as the Pacific Coast, but in depression years the trans-continental tour was not possible. Now with increased interest in the opera has come a demand for presentations in various cities, and there are proposals for lengthening the post season tour. Civic organizations or groups of citizens are willing to subsidize appearances in order that the public may be brought into close personal touch with great operatic performances, and the annual tour may soon bring grand opera to places far distant from New York. Nearby cities such as Philadelphia, Hartford and Newark are visited during the regular season, usually on Tuesday nights when the Opera House itself is dark.

On tour the Metropolitan is virtually an opera house on wheels. For in it are assembled a full cast of artists for the entire repertory, with replacements as a safeguard against emergencies, chorus, ballet, stage crew, with scenery, sets, drops and props. There is generally a carnival spirit about it all. The special train takes on the aspect of a club. The men play bridge or poker, the women read or knit, and the jokes which go into intimate operatic history are perpetrated by the pranksters of the company. The often reported fact that great artists are children at heart is never more clearly evident.

But there are tense moments too, for embarrassing and unexpected emergencies can arise in an out-of-town performance. The Metropolitan sets are frequently too large for other theatres, and must be properly adjusted. The scenery is always shipped a day ahead of time and the stage crew goes to work immediately on arrival. Supers must be recruited locally and the thousand and one possibilities for error in a strange house carefully checked.

For in opera as in the theatre, "the show must go on!"

EQUIPMENT FOR SAFARI

2 special trains
350 artists and staff
500 back drops and tabs
4,000 set pieces
3,500 pieces of lumber
150 boxes of electrical equipment
110 boxes of properties
5,000 complete costumes and accessories
10 trunks of shoes
68 trunks with musical instruments
200 trunks and suitcases

METROPOLITAN OF TOMORROW

TRAILING clouds of glory from its past, the Metropolitan has arrived at its present high achievement. What of its plans for the future?

America today holds a new concept of music—of opera. Through radio, through Guild membership and literature, through the sale of librettos and books on opera, a generation is being educated which will demand great music as a fundamental in every day life. The Metropolitan Opera Association plans to meet this demand.

The Association hopes to stimulate—has in fact already begun to foster a truly national opera for America, one so far reaching that it will touch every section of the country. Its eventual hope is an opera house in every city where local companies will be augmented by visiting stars, and young singers may secure the training so vital to an operatic career. To such a system the Metropolitan, with its list of fine artists, would serve as a great source, as well as an ultimate goal.

The initial steps toward the development of national opera have already been taken. Boston and Philadelphia turn to the Metropolitan annually to present a repertory of their selection. In San Francisco, Baltimore, Cleveland and Rochester; in Chicago, in Cincinnati the promotion of operatic activities has become a civic enterprise, and opera seasons are now permanently established with many Metropolitan artists appearing in leading roles. Each year the road tour meets with increasing response. Smaller opera companies flourish. Opera no longer belongs to the metropolis, but to America.

In addition to fostering such means of helping the ambitious singer, the Metropolitan plans to develop its own American artists. The obligation of the Metropolitan to youth has become increasingly great both because of a new sense of the responsibility of such an institution, and the growing conviction that America must develop its own singers. To this end the Metropolitan is engaging fine artists in advisory capacities, so that out of a complete knowledge of traditional methods America may evolve her own. As part of its plan for a decade ahead, the Association looks forward to a complete modernization of setting and equipment. Since its inception it has been engaged on a building program, assembling within the Metropolitan itself all of the elements which would make possible the finest operatic productions. At first this program was concerned chiefly with personnel—the artists and the reorganization of the various departments, chorus, ballet, orchestra.

Now the problems of the future are concerned with physical equipment. An imperative need for new production, new costumes and settings will arise at the Opera House within the next few years, if performances are to be kept worthy of the company which has been developed. The present warehouse method of storing scenery is awkward and extravagant, since the necessary handling makes new sets appear old before the end of their first season. The importance of production has always been great, but it reaches a climax today because the American audience has grown accustomed to finding its illusion in the most effective and realistic of settings. It has also grown more artistically discriminating and more critical of operatic decor.

So within the next few years the Metropolitan must direct its attention to the establishment of a fund from which such improvements may be financed. It is believed that national interest will make this possible. The Metropolitan is one of the few great opera houses in the world which is not supported by government In France, in Italy, in the Scandinavian countries, demands such as now confront opera in America are met by government or municipal subsidy. But in America the public itself—today's "Patrons of the Opera," must and will maintain the Metropolitan's high standard.

Whether this need will be met in the present house, or in the new theatre which has so long been contemplated can not yet be decided. But that it will be met there can be no question. Out of its glorious past is growing an even greater Metropolitan, a national institution which will present the finest productions and the greatest artists in the world; train young American singers; send stars for guest appearances with local companies in all parts of the country; encourage and present American compositions; make grand opera for all time a basic interest in American life.

OPERA CAVALCADE was written by RUTH ADAMS KNIGHT; cover design by GERSCOVICI; frontispiece by DOHANUS. Photos from ELCAR STUDIOS: Galli-Curci, Manski, Easton, Rothier, Ponselle, Rethberg and Ludikar, Pinza, Bori, Bohnen, List, Schorr, Branzell, Lehmann, Pons, DeLuca, Swarthout, Moore and Tibbett, Chamlee, Bodanzky, Panizza, Pelletier, Flagstad; Parsifal, Götterdämmerung, clowns, Don Giovanni, Lucia di Lammermoor, Lakmé, Bartered Bride, Bruschino, Andrea-Chenier, Elektra, Emperor Jones, Jonny Spielt Auf, Flying Dutchman, Die Meistersinger, Rigoletto, Simon Boccanegra, Parsifal rehearsal, timekeeper, Bohème quartet, Opera House, Fleischer offstage, Rhine maiden rehearsal, orchestra rehearsal, offstage orchestra, backstage serenade; from WIDE WORLD: Brownlee, Edward Ziegler, audience, roof circle, Coq d'Or, Aida super rehearsal, Senz, Tristan set, electrical control, Papi, offstage chorus, Dutchman rehearsal, ballet; from CULVER: Conference, Tetrazzini, Caruso, Fremstad, Schumann-Heink, Chaliapin, Mario, Savage; from ACME: Hempel, Calvé, Melba, Thousands Cheer, Success Story; Caruso drawings, courtesy of LA FOLLIA; photographs of Jean and Edouard De Reszké from the collection of COLONEL CREIGHTON WEBB; charts by THE CHARTMAKERS.